The River

Written by Sarah Gaitanos
Photographs by Brian Enting

The river comes
from the mountains.

The river comes over the rocks.

The river comes past the trees.

The river comes through the city.

The river comes through the park.

The river comes
under the bridge.

The river comes to the sea.